My Friends

By Catherine Bruzzone

Illustrated by Caroline Jayne Church

b small publishing

www.bsmall.co.uk

Your friends

The following pages are for you to fill in lots of details about your friends: friends at school and in the neighbourhood, friends who live far away and even your pets.

You may collect more information, photos or souvenirs than you have room for in this book.

Or you may want to write different things, on separate pieces of paper. If so, here are some ideas for keeping everything together:

You can clip extra paper to the pages, like this:

Or you can make a special envelope on the inside of the back cover, like this:

Cut a triangle from card. Glue or tape it to the back cover.

Or you can make a separate book, like this:

Punch holes in the extra paper. Thread through pieces of wool to hold them together.

To keep your book and extra paper together, tie a ribbon round them, like this:

Now you can read it again when you're older – perhaps with the same friends you write about in the book!

Published by b small publishing ltd.
The Book Shed, 36 Leyborne Park, Kew, Richmond, Surrey, TW9 3HA, UK
www.bsmall.co.uk
Text and illustrations © b small publishing, 1993
This edition published 2013 for Index Books
3   4   5
Printed in China by WKT Co. Ltd.
British Library Cataloguing-in-Publication Data.
A record of this book is available from the British Library.

ISBN-13: 978-1-905710-24-9

First friends

Find the earliest picture of you with a friend or group of friends.

STICK IN PHOTOGRAPH

Me with… _____ Date… _____

Do you still know them? If not, can you find out about them from your parents? How did you meet? Where do they live now? Where do they go to school?

Friends today

Stick in the latest picture of you with a friend or group of friends.

STICK IN PHOTOGRAPH

STICK IN PHOTOGRAPH

Me with… _____ Date…   Me with… _____ Date…

School friends

Name of my school

Draw a plan of your classroom here. Mark where you sit with a **X**.
Can you write in the names of your class?

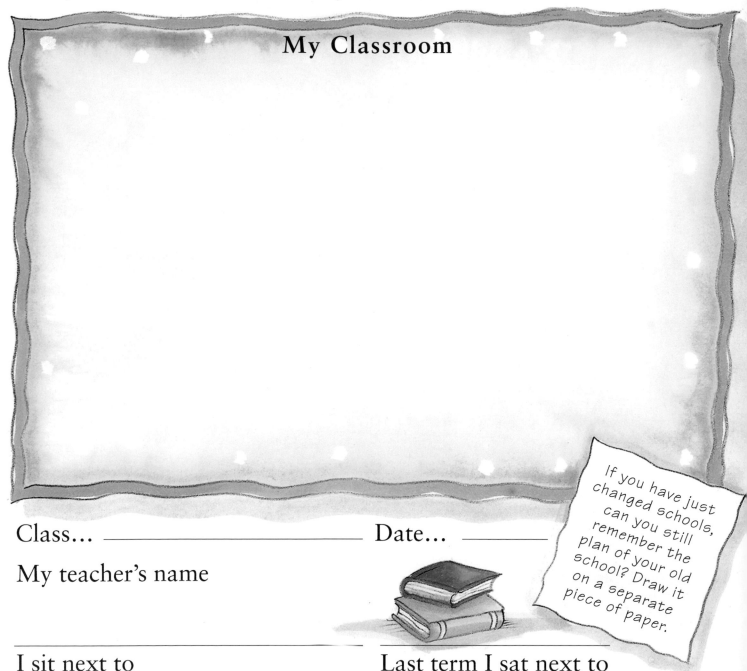

My Classroom

Class... ———————— Date... ————

My teacher's name

I sit next to

Last term I sat next to

If you have just changed schools, can you still remember the plan of your old school? Draw it on a separate piece of paper.

My class

Ask your class to sign their names here.

Autographs

Oldest in the class

_____

Youngest in the class

_____

Friend who lives closest to me

_____

Friends with their birthday in the same month as me

_____

Four school friends

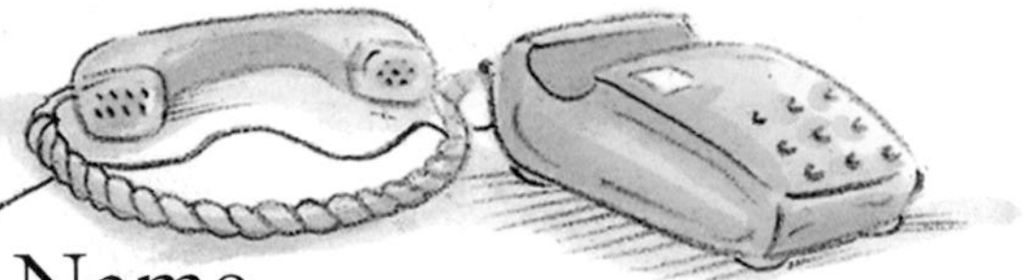

Name

_____

Class

_____

Address

_____

Telephone no.

_____

Birthday

_____

PHOTO

Name

_____

Class

_____

Address

_____

Telephone no.

_____

Birthday

_____

PHOTO

Name

_____

Class

_____

Address

_____

Telephone no.

_____

Birthday

_____

PHOTO

Name

_____

Class

_____

Address

_____

Telephone no.

_____

Birthday

_____

PHOTO

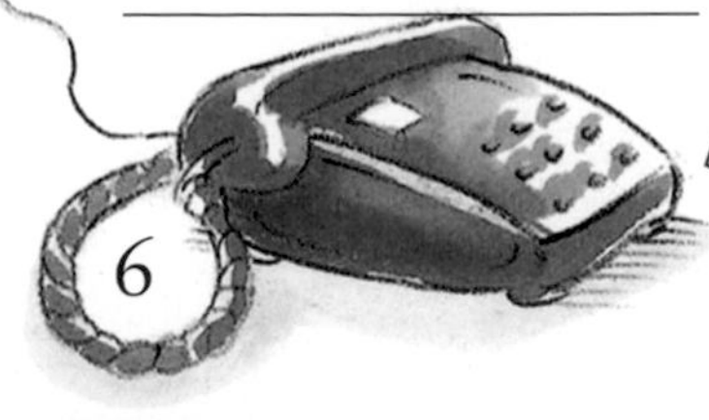

Find a poem about school friends
and copy it out here.

Can you decorate
the poem?
You could draw a
patterned border
or one big picture.
Or you could just
decorate the title
of the poem.

How my friends go to school
Fill in this chart.

Friends	Walk	Car	Bus	Train	Bike

How I go to school _____

Neighbourhood friends

My address

Names of my neighbourhood friends

1   2

Age	Telephone number	Age	Telephone number

This is a map showing where my friends live.

Mark your friends' homes on this map.

MAP

If you have just moved, you could still put the details of your old neighbourhood friends here.

If you live in the country of course, your neighbourhood friends may not live very close

Friendly quiz

Here are 10 general knowledge questions for you and your friends.

1 What is the name of the white bear that lives in the Arctic?

2 How many minutes are there in an hour?

3 Which country do kangaroos come from?

4 What month comes after September?

5 What is the name of the ocean between Europe and North America?

6 A rabbit lives in a…?

7 What is the capital of France?

8 What happens if you freeze water?

9 Which was invented first: the car or the bicycle?

10 The four seasons are: spring, …, autumn, winter?

You can do this quiz with any of your friends, not just your neighbourhood friends. You could use it as a party game too!

Don't peep! Cover these answers while you try the quiz.

Answers

1 polar bear
2 60 minutes
3 Australia
4 October
5 Atlantic
6 burrow or warren
7 Paris
8 it turns to ice
9 the bicycle
10 summer

My best friend

If you don't have a best friend, leave this page. There's lots to fill in on the other pages. If you have more than one special friend, write their details on a separate piece of paper and clip it to this page.

Name

Address

Telephone number

School

Birthday

Sign of the zodiac

Chinese birth sign

Height   Weight

Colour of hair

Colour of eyes

Where and when we met

My friend's favourite...

TV programme...

sport...

book...

food...

film...

sportsperson...

pop star...

What my friend loves doing best in the world!

What my friend hates doing most in the world!

My friend

Draw a picture of your friend here. Or perhaps they could draw a self-portrait for you?

Free time!

Draw a picture here of your favourite playground game. Do you play with friends? Label them on your picture.

My favourite playground game

Games I play in my free time at school

_____

Tick the box if you have a
friend who enjoys...

riding a bike ☐

reading a book ☐

flying a kite ☐

dancing ☐

watching TV ☐

playing a musical instrument ☐

collecting stamps ☐

sewing ☐

making models ☐

singing ☐

drawing and painting ☐

You could also write your friends names. Do you have friends with other pastimes, maybe unusual ones? Why not add them to the list?

Are you in a club or group?

YES ☐   NO ☐

Name of my group

_____

When it meets

_____

Docs it have a symbol?
Draw it here

Names of my friends in the group

_____

What my friends and I like doing
best in the group

This might be a club at school, or a group like Cubs or Brownies. You could start your own club with your friends.

Sports friends

My sports are

Names of friends I meet at sports

1

_____

Sport

_____

2

_____

Sport

Me and my sports friends

STICK IN PHOTOGRAPH

What is the sport?

Who is in the picture?

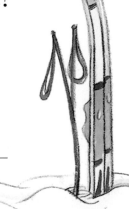

When was it taken?

Pet friends

If you don't have a pet of your own, which pet would you most like to own?

Favourite pet

_____

Pet's name

Pet's picture

Do you have a friend with an unusual pet?

YES   NO

Pet

_____

Friend's name

Do you know anyone with the following pets?

dog ....

cat ....

hamster ....

guinea pig ....

horse or pony ....

insect ....

donkey ....

goldfish ....

snake ....

rabbit ....

bird ....

Write your friends' names here

Penpals

A penpal is a friend you keep in touch with by letter. Often you don't meet your penfriends as they live far away. Maybe you also write to a friend who has moved away? Or a friend you met on holiday? Does your class write to a class in another school?

Ask your penfriend to send you a photo or a souvenir and paste it in here. It could be a stamp, a cinema or bus ticket or a picture she or he has drawn.

STAMP

Do you have a penfriend?

YES ☐   NO ☐

Name

_____

Address

_____

_____

How many letters have you written? ☐

How many letters have you received ☐

My penpal's language

_____

Language we write our letters in

_____

Opposite is a first letter to a penfriend in another country. Imagine you are going to send it. Can you fill it in?

Make up name

Write your address here

Write the date here.

Dear .... and I am .... old.

My name is .... with

I live in .... I am sending you a

.... photograph. My hair is .... and my

eyes are .... I am about

tall and weigh about ....

I go to .... school.

It is about .... kilometre(s) away from my

home and I travel there .... My

favourite pastime is .... and

my favourite sport is ....

Please write and tell me all about yourself.

Love from

If you'd like a penfriend in another country, see if your school can help you find one.

Next time you write to a friend, why not decorate your paper and envelope?

Older friends

Name of my oldest friend

_____

Year when they were born

_____

How much older are they than
you?

.... years

_____

Their work

_____

Place where they were born

_____

Favourite singer when they were
young

_____

Favourite film star when they
were young

_____

Favourite pastime when they
were young

_____

If you have grown-up friends, it is fascinating to find out about life when they were young. They may even be able to show you photograph albums, scrap books and old clothes.

Favourite book when
they were young

_____

Can they remember one famous
event when they were young?

_____

Old fashions!

What did people wear when your oldest friend was young? Draw some examples here and label them. Are they very different from your clothes?

Family friends

Name

Your sister, brother or cousin may be your good friend too! If you want to write about more than one member of your family, use a separate piece of paper and clip it to this page.

Where they live

Favourite food

Relationship to me
(brother, sister, cousin)

Favourite colour

Birthday

Favourite pastime

Height

What I like best about them

Weight

What annoys me about them

Where they go to school

What we like doing together

Holiday friends

Friends I met during my holidays

If you don't go away during the holidays, perhaps you play with different friends at home? Did you go to a care centre or on an outing or a day trip where you met new friends?

If you met lots more friends, write their names, ages and addresses on a separate piece of paper and clip it to this page.

1 Name

Age

Address

Where we met

How we met

What we enjoyed doing together

2 Name

Age

Address

Where we met

How we met

What we enjoyed doing together

STICK IN POSTCARD

Do you have a postcard from your holiday? Stick it in here. Label where or what it is.

A holiday memory
Write a description of a special time you and your friends spent together during the holidays.

Do you have any souvenirs from your holiday: tickets or retaurant bills, foreign coins or sweet wrappers? Stick them here.

Creative friends

These pages are for your friends to fill. Don't forget to ask all your friends to help - and ask new friends too.
It should be fun!

Funny friends
Ask your friends for a funny photo to stick here. They could be making a funny face, or dressed up.

Friendly finger prints
Fill this space with your friends' finger prints. Ask them to sign their names too.

STICK IN PHOTOGRAPH

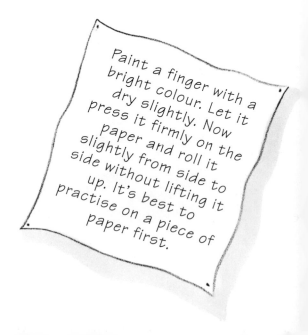

Paint a finger with a bright colour. Let it dry slightly. Now press it firmly on the paper and roll it slightly from side to side without lifting it up. It's best to practise on a piece of paper first.

Joke balloons
Ask your friends to write their favourite jokes here. They can sign their names too.

Friendship flower
Ask each of your friends to write their name on a petal and colour it in with their favourite colour.

23

Forget-me-not

'Souvenir' means 'something to remember'. This page is for you to fill with souvenirs from your friends – so you can always remember them.

Collect something small from each of them: a name tape, a ticket from an outing together, a lock of hair, a joke or rhyme, a passport photograph. Label each souvenir 'From my friend...' and write their name and the date.